ZOOM IN ON BEES

Zoom In on Insects!

Melissa Stewart

Enslow Elementary
an imprint of
Enslow Publishers, Inc.
40 Industrial Road
Box 398
Berkeley Heights, NJ 07922
USA

http://www.enslow.com

CONTENTS

WORDS TO KNOW

colony (KOL uh nee)—A group of animals that lives together.

larva (LAHR vuh)—The second part in the life cycle of some insects. A bee larva is called a grub. A larva changes into a pupa.

nectar (NEK tuhr)—A sugary liquid that many flowers make. Bees and some other insects drink it.

pollen (PAHL uhn)—A sticky powder that must be spread from flower to flower for plants to make seeds. Bees and some other insects eat it.

pupa (PYOO puh)—The third part in the life cycle of some insects. A pupa changes into an adult.

3

BEE HOMES

ZOOM BUBBLE

Bees live all over the world. Many bees live alone. They dig holes in the ground or tunnel into wood.

Other bees live in large groups. A group of bees is called a colony. A colony can have more than fifty thousand bees.

PARTS OF A BEE

wings

thorax

head

antennae

abdomen

eye

legs

BEE BODY

A bee is an insect. An insect has six legs. Its body has three main parts.

An insect's head is in the front. The thorax is in the middle. The abdomen is the part at the back.

BEE EYES

ZOOM BUBBLE

You can see two large eyes on this bee. They help the bee see colors and shapes.

A bee also has three small eyes. They are between the large eyes. A bee's small eyes can tell if it is day or night.

BEE ANTENNAE

ZOOM BUBBLE

A bee has two long antennae (an TEN ee) on its head. They help a bee feel, hear, smell, and taste. A bee can also taste with its mouth and front feet.

BEE TONGUES

ZOOM BUBBLE

Most bees get their food from flowers. They sip sweet, sugary nectar with their long tongues. Nectar gives bees energy.

Bees eat pollen, too. It helps them stay healthy and strong.

BEE WINGS

ZOOM BUBBLE

A bee has two sets of wings. It beats them more than two hundred times a second as it whizzes through the air. Now that's fast!

BEE LEGS

ZOOM BUBBLE

A bee has six legs. The legs are attached to the middle of the body.

Bees that live in colonies have tiny baskets on their legs. They use the baskets to carry pollen back to their nest.

This bee just stung a person.
It left its stinger in the skin.

BEE STINGER

Look at this bee's back end.
See the sharp, hollow stinger?
When the bee feels angry
or scared, it attacks. It jabs
the stinger into its enemy.
Then it pumps poison into
the wound. Ouch!

BEE GRUBS

ZOOM BUBBLE

When a bee comes
out of its egg, it looks
like a little white worm.
It is called a grub.

A bee grub eats and eats.
After about five days, it is
ready to become a pupa.

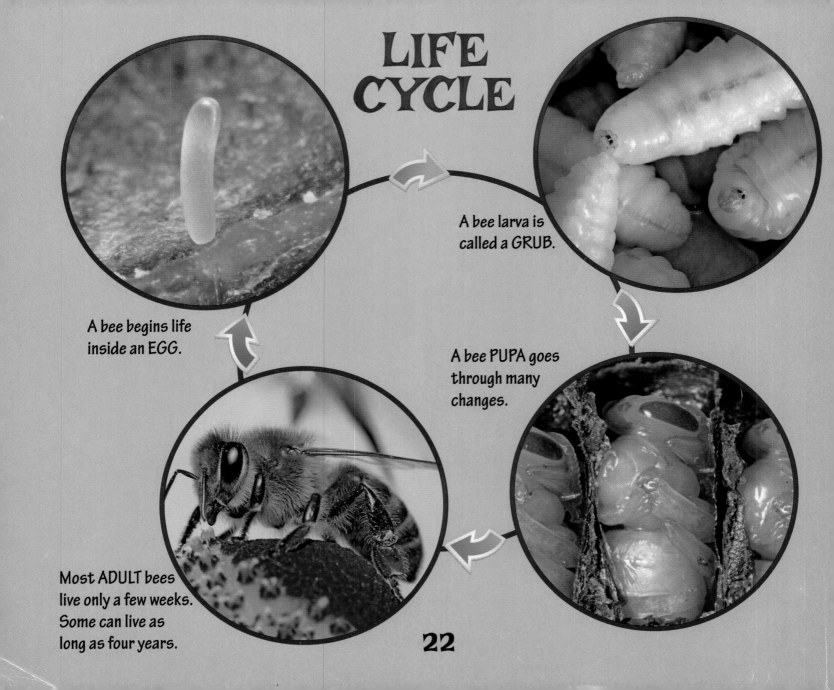

LIFE CYCLE

A bee begins life inside an EGG.

A bee larva is called a GRUB.

A bee PUPA goes through many changes.

Most ADULT bees live only a few weeks. Some can live as long as four years.

22

LEARN MORE

BOOKS

Peterson, Megan Cooley. *Look Inside A Bee Hive.* Mankato, Minn.: Capstone Press, 2012.

Rotner, Shelley, and Anne Woodhull. *The Buzz on Bees: Why Are They Disappearing?* New York: Holiday House, 2010.

Sayre, April Pulley. *The Bumblebee Queen.* Watertown, Mass.: Charlesbridge, 2005.

WEB SITES

San Diego Zoo Kids. *Bees.*
<http://kids.sandiegozoo.org/animals/insects/bee>

National Geographic Kids. *Honeybees.*
<http://kids.nationalgeographic.com/kids/animals/creaturefeature/honeybees>

INDEX

Enslow Elementary, an imprint of Enslow Publishers, Inc.
Enslow Elementary® is a registered trademark of Enslow Publishers, Inc.

Copyright © 2014 by Melissa Stewart

Library of Congress Cataloging-in-Publication Data

Stewart, Melissa.
 Zoom in on bees / Melissa Stewart.
   p. cm. — (Zoom in on insects)
 Summary: "Provides information for readers about a bee's home, food, and body"—Provided by publisher.
  ISBN 978-0-7660-4210-0
 1. Bees—Juvenile literature. I. Title. II. Series: Stewart, Melissa. Zoom in on insects.
 QL565.2.S74 2014
 595.799—dc23

                    2012040386

Future editions:
Paperback ISBN: 978-1-4644-0363-7
EPUB ISBN: 978-1-4645-1201-8
Single-User PDF ISBN: 978-1-4646-1201-5
Multi-User PDF ISBN: 978-0-7660-5833-0

Printed in the United States of America
102013 Lake Book Manufacturing, Inc. Melrose Park, IL
10 9 8 7 6 5 4 3 2 1

Photo Credits: © Alex Wild, p. 22 (top left); Dr. Jeremy Burgess/Science Source, pp. 13, 18; Eric Isselée/Photos.com, p. 3; © iStockphoto.com/HAIBO BI, pp. 21, 22 (top right); Moeed Hussain/Photos.com, p. 15; Scott Camazine/Science Source, p. 16; Shutterstock.com, pp. 1, 2, 4, 5, 6, 7, 8, 9, 10, 11, 12, 14, 17, 22 (bottom left); © Stephen Dalton/Minden Pictures, p. 22 (bottom right); Steve Gschmeissner/Science Source, p.19; © WILDLIFE GmbH/Alamy, p. 20.

Cover Photo: Shutterstock.com

Series Literacy Consultant:
Allan A. De Fina, PhD
Past President of the New Jersey Reading Association
Dean, College of Education
New Jersey City University
Jersey City, New Jersey

Science Consultant:
Helen Hess, PhD
Professor of Biology
College of the Atlantic
Bar Harbor, Maine